MULTIDIMENSIONAL ASPECTS-HIGHER SELVES

GALACTIC GRANDMOTHER SPIRITUAL JOURNEY SERIES

APRIL AUTRY

COPYRIGHT © 2020

A Rights Reserved

No part of this book shall be reproduced or transmitted in any form or by any means without prior written permission of the publisher. No liability is assumed for damages resulting from the use of the information contained herein. The information within this book is presented from the author's personal experience and perspective, to assist the reader's quest for spiritual enlightenment and well-being, Neither the author nor the publisher assumes any responsibility for errors, omissions, or contrary interpretations of the subject matter herein. Any perceived slight of any individual or organization is purely unintentional.

GALACTIC GRANDMOTHER®

https://GalacticGrandmother.com
https://info@galacticgrandmother.com

ISBN (ebook) 978-1-954785-007

ALSO BY APRIL AUTRY

Galactic Grandmother Past Life Series

ATLANTIS, JOURNEY FROM THE INNER TEMPLE

MY LIFE WITH JESUS

ESCAPE FROM MALDEK.

Galactic Grandmother Spiritual Journey Series

WORKING IN THE QUANTUM FIELD, BOOK 1 & 2

PROLOGUE

Multidimensionality is a complex subject. Immediately we are into drawn into concepts of the quantum field, where linear time does not exist, multiple aspects of our Self do exist, and these aspects exist concurrently on varying energetic levels. A simpler way of saying this, is that we have aspects of ourself or higher selves that currently live in higher dimensions. This book shares experiences I have had with my higher aspects until now.

As you will learn, I have strong ties to the Lemurian people through past life experiences, through current lives of my higher aspects, and myself in this timeline. In my case, those ties overlap with the work I do for the Lemurians.

IT'S WELL DOCUMENTED that we are energy, and everything in our world from a chair to plants are also energy. From a spiritual perspective, this energy originates from our Divine Creator, God, Mother-Father God, however you wish to label it. Our Creator Source energy is infinite, eternal and 100%

love energy, whether the energy is used to create a chair, plant, human or extraterrestrial being.

Our spirit guides, which may appear as angels, ascended masters, a religious figure, or beings of light, are usually at first perceived to be outside of us. As we learn more about our multidimensionality, we realize that our spirit guides are often our higher selves appearing in a way that we are comfortable with. I say selves or aspects in pleural, because we have many other versions of us within the quantum field. As we expand our consciousness, and raise our energetic frequency, it is possible to communicate with them.

Our spiritual support team may also include angels, ascended masters, or extraterrestrials that are not our higher aspects, so it is import to distinguish between different kinds of energetic beings. Learning energetic discernment is a lesson everyone goes through at some point in their evolution. This is especially important when lower energetic beings, try to masquerade as higher energetic beings, in an attempt to influence you.

MY MAIN SPIRIT guide is a higher aspect of myself, and checks in on me daily, at least once and very often multiple times. I am in alignment with my higher Self, so when I close my eyes with the intention of connecting and breath into my heart space, I receive messages from my guide that begin with "we." We would have you do this, or we would have you do that. Usually my messages are related to the Galactic Grandmother projects, however if I have a personal concern or question, I receive counseling, a download of pertinent information, or an interactive teaching. The interactive teachings often take me via my light body somewhere.

AS BEINGS OF ENERGY, we are fractals of our Divine Creator, which gives us infinite Creator abilities. Just as we are able to live concurrent lives on different dimensions, we are able to live concurrent lives during the same timeline. In my case, I am aware that I lived both as a man and woman during the time of Jesus. In this current lifetime I live as the woman April, while a man born on the same day and time as myself yet in a different location, lives his life currently unaware of me.

I know his first name, where he lives, yet we will never meet. I learned about my masculine counterpart through meditation, when I found myself inside this man's consciousness. I felt his emotions, saw the women in his life, and experienced his thoughts as he navigated through a lesson at that time. He is a handsome older man, successful and married to a woman he loves. However, his wife's sex drive had decreased with time, and this man took a younger mistress. He was evaluating his priorities, when I popped into his consciousness, and I followed his thoughts to the decision that he would break-up with his mistress. He decided that his wife and marriage were his priorities.

This was interesting, yet my first question was, "Why am I inside this man's head?"

I received the download that living concurrent lives as masculine and feminine, is an expedited way to clear karma, heal, and gain wisdom.

We are multidimensional beings, with an infinite spiritual nature, and are capable of more than we can imagine.

At this time in humanities' evolution, we need to expand our awareness of who we are and what comes naturally to us. Our collective future is beautiful, yet people must have an open mind, so that new ideas can be considered.

If you have not previously considered yourself as multidimensional, my hope is that you allow seeds to be planted, and have confidence that your Higher Self will guide you to a fuller understanding.

1. **ARTHUR**

A friend asked me to accompany her, for an appointment with a doctor, that now worked solely as an energy healer. My friend wanted me to take notes about her healing session, which was expected to last approximately two hours. I was eager to see how an energy healer worked, and what modalities would be used. Although this energy healer was educated as a Doctor of Chiropractic, she did not use her hands to adjust my friend, instead she used kinetic muscle testing to ask questions and receive answers.

My friend was asked to lay on a massage table, and on the wall next to her, were charts of possible areas that needed healing. The charts covered topics such as old emotional wounds, soul contracts, and energy attachments. The doctor used not only the client's answers from muscle testing, she used her own intuition, and she worked with healers in the spiritual dimensions as well as the client's spiritual team. Most interesting to me, was when the doctor spoke of working with extraterrestrial healers.

After the doctor began working, she mentioned an Arcturian healer named Arthur, had come in to help her do clearing and heal my friend. After watching the doctor work for two hours, she asked Arthur if he had a message for my friend, before she ended the session. To everyone's surprise, Arthur told the doctor that he wanted me to relay his message. I sat in the corner of the room, with my mouth open, as the doctor asked me if I could do this. I told her that I would try and closed my eyes to quiet my mind. I heard a simple message in my mind, which I relayed, and my friend's session came to an end.

I justified to myself, that the reason Arthur asked me to relay the message, was because I had recently realized I was telepathic. The voice that I heard in my mind, that sounded like my own voice, was indeed telepathic communication. I was hearing from my higher Self, yet at that time, I believed I was hearing from an external angel or guide. This voice validated itself, by foretelling things that happened later, so I sought better alignment by meditating daily.

FOLLOWING my friend's healing session, I sat on my couch to meditate, and was perplexed. I believed that when we die, our spirit leaves our body, and goes into a higher dimension. A place where there is a great library, and gardens, and where one meets up with friends and family that have already passed. I believed that we had spirit guides from that dimension that help us, and I believed that angels also help us. I believed in Ascended Masters, such as Jesus and Buddha, that had attained spiritual mastery, and continue to assist humanity. And I believed in God, not a personified figure on a throne, but a vague creator that was behind all that exists. I believed God to be in charge of karma, reincarnation, and all things good and bad. Yet believing all this, I had not considered the idea of beings from other planets, and found it hard to understand how extraterrestrials, like the Arcturian healer Arthur, played into spirituality.

So, I sat on my couch wondering about this, and asked a simple question.

"Help me understand."

I asked my question to no one in particular, I just knew I didn't have the full picture, and needed help. I closed my eyes, breathed slowly, and let my mind become quiet. I looked into the darkness behind my eyelids and relaxed.

"This is Arthur. I am with you and will help you understand."

I heard this in my mind, in what sounded like my own voice. I remained quiet, and a picture came into my mind. I was far away in space, looking down at planet Earth. Then Arthur began to tell me what I was seeing. I saw a layer of silver-grey clouds, as thick as Earth was wide, and the clouds surrounded Earth.

"This is your fourth dimension." Arthur told me. "This holds Earth's energy, and when your body dies, your spirit comes here."

I looked at this thick silver cloud surrounding the Earth and understood that what I believed about life after death belonged here.

"This dimension has many levels and holds all of Earth's beliefs about spirituality and God. The fourth dimension holds the energy of your home, so when you are between lives, you still feel connected to all that you know." Arthur said.

This made sense to me. I intuitively knew that this was also where we went, while our bodies slept. I admired this view of Earth, surrounded by the thick layer of the fourth dimension, and realized that I was seeing it from space. The space that an extraterrestrial such as Arthur, would look down from. I got the sense of dimensions beyond the fourth, then it was gone. I opened my eyes, and was amazed at what I had seen, and realized about life after death.

"Arthur," I said out loud, "I will meditate every morning, and I ask that you show me more."

THE NEXT MORNING when I meditated, I felt a tingling around my chin, and learned this was Arthur's energy. Other than that, I only remember feeling love and an overwhelming peace. The following day as I began my meditation, I felt the tingling around my chin, and knew Arthur was with me. I then asked the question, which would begin my path to true awakening.

"Arthur," I asked in my mind, "Who are you?"

I heard the answer as clear as you are reading these words.

"I am you." Arthur answered.

"Me?" I asked incredulously.

"You are multidimensional," Arthur answered, "I am a higher aspect of you."

"I'm Arcturian?" I uttered.

"Everyone may know their true lineage," Arthur told me, "if they want to."

My meditation ended abruptly. My mind was blown.

"Have I lost my mind?" I thought, "have I finally gone over the edge?"

The thought of an Arcturian named Arthur, being a higher aspect of myself, wasn't something I could comprehend.

"I'm Arcturian!" I said out loud.

For the next week, I was obsessed with this thought. I

didn't understand it, I had never heard of such a thing, and I seriously doubted my sanity. Maybe I was just hearing nonsense in my head, yet I couldn't deny the picture of Earth surrounded by the cloud of fourth dimensional energy, and the intuitive knowing that what Arthur told me about the fourth dimension was true.

My neat little package of understanding had been shattered. I hit the internet with a vengeance. I typed in Arcturian and was astonished to find a lot of people claim to be Arcturian. I began to read everything I could, about people that know their extraterrestrial heritage, or were in communication with extraterrestrials. I found Peter Maxwell Slattery on YouTube, read about James Gilliland at ECETI in Washington, and learned about an American Indian woman, Tashina, that said she was also Arcturian. All these testimonies helped me understand that I was not alone. Gradually, I grasped the concept that I was multidimensional.

The next year I attended ECETI's weekend conference, which included lectures by James Gilliland, Tashina, and a Galactic Medicine Wheel Ceremony. We learned about extraterrestrials, and I looked forward to a night sky watch, where we might see their ships. Although the sky watch was cancelled, due to rain and clouds, I did get a reading from Tashina, and she told me about Arthur. In her own words:

"He's worked with the Orions, he's worked with the Arcturians so he carries some of that energy, he likes the Andromedans quite a bit. He's a higher level planetary spiritual ambassador, but more of the Orions, and actually Arthur is an incorrect name. This particular energetic form from Creator Source carries a balanced male-female energy. He's

so highly evolved that he doesn't care what you call him, but you may choose a name that has an energetic representation of what he is. His shows himself as two balls of light, one is above and one is anchored into you. He is bringing in energies to you. From the Andromedans he is bringing in very specific intellectual, factual knowledge. From the Arcturians he's bringing in the spiritual awareness you had, but you seem to be awakening to and tapping into more lately. He's a very old, old energy and will help you write your book. The purpose of the book is to facilitate people to do soul healing, reconnective healing, and reconnecting with who they are."

Years later I received a download that Arthur agreed to be the intermediary between my Higher Self that is my main spiritual guide and me. Being introduced to Arthur, by a doctor that vetted his authenticity, was the best way to eliminate doubts that would have come up otherwise. Arthur isn't my higher aspect, yet because my main guide carried a lot of Arcturian energy, my guide was able to step in for a connection with me. In a sense, Arthur worked as a channel for my guide.

I CONTINUE to be astounded by the perfection of planning, timing, and execution by my Higher Selves on my behalf. My spiritual enlightenment has been marked by synchronicity and by being carefully led down a path toward my next aha moment. Ideas drop into my head, or are given directly in meditation, and off I go toward further expansion of my consciousness.

I envision my Self here in the third dimension, as the smallest aspect of who I am. Rising above into the fourth, fifth and higher dimensions, I understand I experience life in different forms, expanding my consciousness until I reunite with my Divine Creator Source. I am also open to the fact that just as my little package of understanding was shattered when Arthur introduced himself, I will continue to expand my awareness by new concepts presented to me.

We are fortunate, no matter what circumstances we find ourselves in, to be able to go within and explore who we are. This adventure is really peeling away the layers of the persona we have acquired, so that we find our authentic Self. True happiness and excellent health are directly proportional to the amount of effort and success we have in knowing ourselves. At our core, we are 100% love and creativity.

Be excited! You are awesome! You are a valuable asset to humanity, and I am grateful for you being here.

2. LOVE

The highest aspect of myself that I am aware of, my main spiritual guide, was introduced to me through an Arcturian healer named Arthur. A reading I received from Tashina, an American Indian woman and Arcturian consciousness presently incarnated, confirmed details of who my main guide is and how he helps me. I gave her reading in the last chapter so I will continue my story after that.

Tashina told me *"He's so highly evolved that he doesn't care what you call him, but you may choose a name that has an energetic representation of what he is."*

How do I name a beautifully balanced energetic Being, that lovingly guides me, and gives me what I need to carry out my life's mission? Any name that I choose, must be imbued with the energy of unselfish service, and worthy of that Being's commitment to me. So, what name did I pick? Love. Yes, Love. The universal energy of the Creator. Because to me, the Being now named Love, represents all I am evolving toward, and the possibility of unlimited potential.

From 2014 when Arthur, aka Love, first contacted me in meditation until now, I have undergone an accelerated education about multidimensionality. Love has guided me through realization after realization of who I am, about our origins on this planet, the influences of both dark and light forces in our current collective consciousness, and where we are headed.

Love has given me guidance, emotional support, and insights about my life and who I am. In 2016 he tasked me with my first writing assignment, and has continued to request that I write books about my spiritual journey and many of my past lives. By sharing what I have learned, an energetic pathway is forged for others.

Love has been the director for all the Galactic Grandmother projects, including the website GalacticGrandmother.com, as a platform to assist the collective's ascension to a higher consciousness.

3. **TARA**

I met my friend when I traveled to Mt Shasta, California for a spiritual retreat. She and I recognized each other immediately. She thought that she must have seen me around town, and I thought I probably saw her on a YouTube video. Even though we looked familiar to each other, we found that we had never met. When it was time for me to leave Mt Shasta, we promised to stay in touch, as she lived in Mt Shasta, and I lived in San Diego.

Just two months later, my friend called and asked me if I would accompany her to Sedona, Arizona for a conference. We spent the road trip to Sedona telling each other about our lives. It was as if we already knew each other and were catching up.

The fall weather in Sedona was warm and sunny with beautiful blue skies, just perfect to enjoy brunch in a restaurant's outdoor patio. She excused herself to use the restroom, and after she left, I suddenly saw a vision of us. We were wearing form fitting, silver body suits, looked about thirty years old, and she had long blonde hair while I had long brown hair.

Currently, she does have long blonde hair, and I used to have long brown hair before it turned silver. In my vision, I knew that we were aboard a spaceship, that we were best friends discussing our next incarnation, and when we would meet up. This vision explained the fact that we recognized each other immediately, that we felt a close connection, and wanted to know about each other's lives.

THIS VISION WAS my introduction to Tara. Tara is my higher aspect that currently lives and works aboard a Pleiadian mother ship. She is an Ambassador for the Lemurian city of Telos, the interdimensional city within Mt Shasta. This Pleiadian mother ship has ambassadors from many star nations that live and work aboard, and hosts intergalactic council meetings, which Tara attends.

My friend's higher aspect also lives and works aboard the Pleiadian ship. We have incarnated into the third dimension as soul family, to support each other personally and professionally, and to assist humanity during ascension.

Tara has shown me how she channels to me. When I am typing on my computer, she is also typing on hers, and her words and thoughts come directly through to me. For us to have the best possible connection, she downloaded some of her energy into me. I will never forget this experience, because she was also consciously connected to me for about twelve hours. I didn't realize we were consciously connected, until I stepped outside. She was with me in my mind, and I could hear her thoughts about what she was experiencing through me.

"It's so beautiful! The trees, the plants, and feeling the ground as you walk." Tara exclaimed.

I walked toward my car, and she continued.

"Oh!" She said with glee, "I get to drive an antique!"

I laughed at this comment as I got into my car. I turned on the car and backed out of my parking space. Tara was excited and having fun as we drove on the street. That trip was like an old-time amusement park ride to her!

I HAVE strong ties to Telos, the city that Tara represents. The year prior to meeting Tara, I became obsessed with learning about Telos. One day as I sat reading a book about Telos, I had a visitation from the High Priest Adama of Telos. He flashed into my room, with someone else standing next to him, and relayed the message that I would be working with him. Then he was gone. I got very excited about traveling to Mt Shasta after that.

Later, I would realize the reason that Hawaii feels like home to me, is because I spent a very long time reincarnating there. The islands of Hawaii, are what remains of the highest mountains on the continent of Mu, before it sank. Mu was home to the Lemurians, and prior to Mu sinking, approximately 25,000 Lemurians escaped to Mt Shasta. The Lemurians were spiritually advanced and built the interdimensional city of Telos inside Mt Shasta. I then incarnated to Telos, because I loved the Lemurian culture and spirituality, and have met another of my aspects that currently resides there.

4. ARAYA

I have taken many shamanic journeys to Telos in my light body. When I arrive there, I am greeted by my animal companion, Bela, an adult female lion. Her eyes shine golden brown, and she has a beautiful, soft, shiny coat of medium brown. During a previous incarnation in Telos, I was a young man and Bela bonded with my soul. Since then, she has remained my animal companion in all my incarnations there. She is a higher dimensional, independent being who chooses to be with me, and we love each other.

All animals are vegetarians in Telos and co-exist in peace with other animals and people. Bela and I are inseparable when I am in Telos, we lay on the grass in the park together, she follows me to the spa, and she is allowed to follow me into the temple. I cannot describe the trust and love between us, yet I know that other animal lovers feel this with their companion animals.

During a visit to Telos, Bela and I went into the Feminine Temple, where a meditation was being led by Priestess ARaya. I walked through the center aisle, with benches on either side filled with people, and reached the raised platform where the priestess stood. The priestess was older with short white hair, and she wore a long blue dress. Suddenly, I was inside the priestess, looking out at the people in the temple. I was sharing her consciousness, just as Tara had shared mine. I got to experience this meditation through the priestess leading it. I looked out from her eyes at the men and women sitting in the temple, listened to the words she spoke, and was inside her head.

I heard the priestess lead the group in a meditation to open their heart portal, go up their soul streams, balance their Divine Masculine and Divine Feminine energies, and expand their high heart center so they could channel love directly down their soul streams from Source. The meditation was ended by sending loving energy, as a group, out to the collective consciousness. This meditation was called a High Heart Expansion and lasted a full forty-five minutes of my shamanic journey. As the priestess ended the meditation, I was called back from my journey.

After this amazing experience, Love told me that I would be leading the same meditation as Priestess ARaya. I had not known the priestess's name until then, yet there was a familiarity about her. I told Love that I would need help remembering what she said, and within a week I received the download of the meditation.

MY FRIEND and I went to Sedona for a second time together, and during this visit I went on another shamanic journey to Telos. During this journey I walked through the Feminine temple, into the garden behind the temple, where I saw

Adama the High Priest of Telos, standing next to a fountain. I walked to him and he smiled, then put his hand into the water of the fountain and placed a wet finger on the center of my forehead.

Adama transferred thoughts to me that ARaya is my aspect living in Telos, and because ARaya and I are both 5D consciousness, I was now fully integrated with her. I put my hand up, to see her light body merge with my hand, and knew that we were one. I then saw my Divine Masculine partner, a Priest in the Masculine temple, walk to me through the garden and we embraced.

Adama showed me that ARaya is a leader among the Galactic Grandmothers, that she gathers them together, and trains them as a part of her personal responsibilities. I was told that ARaya is my name when performing Galactic Grandmother duties. The following day I led the High Heart Expansion Meditation in Sedona as ARaya April.

Even though Tara had downloaded energy to me, this experience of fully integrating and merging with an energetically matched aspect was unique. My friend and I agreed that we are learning by doing, and soon after, my friend also integrated her 5D aspect.

SINCE INTEGRATION WITH PRIESTESS ARAYA, when I travel to Telos in my light body, I become one with her. I go to her home, swim in her pool and enjoy the higher frequency energy there. She has since come into me when I am doing healing sessions. She literally takes over the session, speaking to the client in a beautiful soothing voice, while she runs energy through them. Priestess ARaya has taught me how to do energy healing sessions that I never knew before. I don't know if this is a fair exchange, with me and Bela lounging around her pool and her performing healing sessions, but it seems to work for us so far!

5. **TIAMAT**

While in meditation, I was shown myself walking outside. I stood tall and strong, with short platinum blonde hair that shined brightly under the sun. After seeing this image of myself, for the next year and a half, I was obsessed with trying to look like this. I had my hair cut short, had it bleached blonde, and increased my gym workouts. The blonde hair color was never right until I let my natural silver grow out, and that was the platinum color I had seen shining under the sun. During this time, I asked why I saw myself looking like this, and why was I so obsessed with it. I channeled the following information.

"*This transmission is from your Higher Self, Tiamat. You are a channel for the Great Cosmic Mother, and as such, you represent all aspects of her Divinity. Tiamat is one such aspect. Tiamat has been maligned due to the Mesopotamia mythology, and it is now time to enlighten humanity to the*

part Tiamat actually played on Earth, and in humanity's spiritual development.

Tiamat is the creative Force/Power from the black void of the Great Cosmic Mother. In mythology Tiamat came from an angry sea and produced all, yet this is only partially the truth. Yes, the great cosmic void of the Mother is black and infinite, yet it is calm and is the breath of Love. The breath of love for ALL. When the Great Cosmic Father brings the light of an idea, then the Great Cosmic Mother manifests the idea from her infinite womb of creation.

Tiamat is the force and power of creation's manifestation (Divine Feminine) that is equal to the power and light of creation's ideas (Divine Masculine). In ancient times, and for many reasons, mankind feared because they did not understand their place within the whole. Mankind was used, and manipulated by extraterrestrials that presented themselves as Gods, and promoted self-serving agendas. The Great Cosmic Mother and Father's creative energy is neutral and ONLY loving, and is responsible for all, including the extraterrestrials. This was not understood by mankind. Mythology put Tiamat in the category with other Gods of that time, and Tiamat was given personality traits that were feared.

With humanity's consciousness ascending, it is time to understand this aspect of the Great Cosmic Mother named Tiamat. On Earth there is an image of Divine Feminine energy associated with the Great Cosmic Mother, in which a feminine woman with long flowing hair is revered for her motherly love and compassion, as well as her sexuality and sexual powers to manifest. This image holds truth, and is also associated with the Earth Mother mythology, yet it is only one aspect of the Great Cosmic Mother.

Tiamat is the original Goddess, she is the original Mother, she is the original womb of creation. Just as man *mixes his physical sperm with a woman's egg in the womb, so that she may manifest a child and give it birth, Tiamat is the black void that receives light from the Cosmic Father, then uses that light to manifest an idea and give it birth.*

Tiamat is here to walk amongst us and reintroduce herself in a new form. The great mysteries will be known to All once again. Love and abundance are mankind's inheritance. Tiamat is here to help guide us to our Divine nature and unite us with the joy of what we truly are.

Our vessel April was shown an image of herself as Tiamat in this modern age. Tiamat stood tall, strong, equally integrated with Divine Masculine and Feminine energies, enlightened, and a loving vessel of the Great Cosmic Mother's Love. Tiamat walked under the sun and her hair was short and bright platinum. April knew she was seeing an aspect of herself yet did not know who this aspect represented until three months later. April was given the name Tiamat, and she did not know who Tiamat was, yet she was obsessed with looking like her.

April is a Galactic Grandmother, and like other Galactic Grandmothers, will represent the version of Tiamat that is now aligned with our consciousness. Other Galactic Grandmothers will show Tiamat in many physical forms, yet for April, we chose that she should paint a new image of the Great Cosmic Mother into the collective consciousness. Younger generations already choose a rainbow of colors to decorate their hair, and we wanted to honor their freedom of expression and authenticity. The new version of Tiamat is a systems buster in all ways."

Tiamat is that aspect of the Great Cosmic Mother that all souls align with through the Divine Feminine energies. We all are aspects of Tiamat, as well as, aspects that represent the Great Cosmic Father and Divine Masculine energies. We have spent countless incarnations with the goal of balancing these energies. My personal experience of seeing myself as Tiamat, anchored my consciousness into the knowing, that our Divine Creators' energies are equally powerful and work together in perfect harmony.

6. HAALAH

One morning I was in the kitchen preparing my coffee. I put water in the electric kettle, and coffee in my French press, when suddenly a dish towel fell to the floor from the handle of the dishwasher. I picked up the towel and hung it back up, turned off the electric kettle, made my coffee and left the kitchen. After finishing my coffee, I returned to the kitchen and found the towel on the floor again, so I hung it up and turned away. When I turned back, the towel was on the floor!

"Who's here with me?" I asked.

The water kettle turned on by itself, and water began boiling. I got strong goose bumps on my legs and Nefertiti came into my mind, also the words "sex magic."

"Wow!" I thought, "She really knows how to make an entrance!"

Later in meditation, I received the following information.

∼

When I dedicated my life to service of others, it opened up new fields of my knowledge. My higher aspect that lived during Neferiti's time, and who was involved in the secret schools of Egypt, will work with me to bring forth knowledge from the secret schools. She will teach me about manipulating energy for the good and benefit of the All this time. Sex magic is energetic knowledge of manifestation by the Great Cosmic Mother. This higher aspect will assist in bringing the dark magic into the light, so it is attached to the We consciousness. The door will be opened and "We will take your hand and lead the way."

I had not heard from my Nefertiti aspect for ten months, when she contacted me during meditation. She gave me her name, which is Haalah. She told me that I can use magic/alchemy like that of prayer, with good intentions to surround people with blankets of love energy, so that they feel loved and secure. She said this work is done in the quantum field. Haalah told me that she had another life as a woman that followed Jesus during his teaching years. She used this technique to anchor higher vibrational energies that supported Jesus and his mission.

This information was very interesting to me, because I remember and have written about a past life, in which I was a man named Samuel that followed Jesus/Yeshua during his ministry. According to what Haalah said, we were in female and male bodies, experiencing from the feminine and masculine perspectives, during the same timeline.

In this current lifetime, my oversoul is doing the same. I am experiencing from the feminine perspective of April, and also from the masculine perspective of a man born on the same day.

7. **LARK**

While writing a past life experience about escaping Maldek, and becoming a refugee on the continent of Mu, I realized that the community I was writing about did not match my memories of Lemuria. The buildings were more modern, as was the culture of the community we were living in. I felt something was off, so prior to a shamanic journey, I made the intention to learn how it was that I settled on Mu yet was not living the Lemurian lifestyle.

Upon entering the meditative state during my shamanic journey, I felt my light body being taken away. I asked where I was going and was given the name "Venus." Upon arriving there, I was greeted by a tall, attractive woman with long blonde hair, wearing a beige dress that reached the floor, in what looked like a coarse material like linen. She told me that Venusians were in resonance to the native Lemurians, because both had 5D and above consciousness. Because of this, the Galactic Council had approved Venus to build colonies on the continent of Mu, and one of these Venusian colonies was chosen as the best place for refugees from

Maldek to settle. I asked her who she was and was told that she is my higher aspect on Venus, and that her name is Lark.

While I intuitively felt this information was true, and it certainly answered my questions about the community I was writing about, I had never heard of colonies from Venus on Mu. I was then guided to a video on YouTube by Omnec Onec, who claims to be from Venus. In her video she speaks of Venusian colonies on Mu, and that was the external confirmation I needed to know the information I received was indeed correct.

FINAL THOUGHTS

These are only a few of my higher frequency multidimensional aspects. These higher selves stepped forward to help me during this incarnation, and I am grateful for their guidance.

I have written about many topics that are definitely outside the 3D perspective, besides our higher selves or aspects, the concept of feminine and masculine aspects living during the same lifetime, may be something new to consider.

If we have multiple selves living concurrently within the quantum field on different bands of frequency, and we can have energy and information downloaded from those higher selves, why could we not also have downloaded energy into two bodies here in this now timeline to accomplish accelerated enlightenment? We are spiritual beings, multidimensional spiritual beings, and we are just scratching the surface of what our true potential is. We need to blow open the box that our small human mind has kept our consciousness caged in and allow for truth to find its way to us. We need only to say the words,

"I am ready to know who I am."

ABOUT THE AUTHOR

April Autry

April writes about her spiritual journey, including many of her past lives.

April is an intuitive mentor, Quantum healer, Reiki master, yoga teacher, and teaches alignment of your mind-body-soul through consciousness expansion and spiritual practices.

April's books and products can be found on her website:

https://GalacticGrandmother.com

April enjoys reading your book reviews, so please feel free to email her at:

https://info@galacticgrandmother.com